Library of Congress Control Number: 2012935527

ISBN 978-93-8982-395-0

Edited by Cassandra Pelham
Creative Director: David Saylor
Book Design by Phil Falco and Kazu Kibuishi

First edition: September 2012
This edition: November 2022

Printed in India

BOOK FIVE
PRINCE OF THE ELVES

AN IMPRINT OF

SCHOLASTIC

YOU'VE NEVER HEARD ABOUT THE GREAT ERLKING?

THE STORIES ABOUT HIM ARE SO AMAZING.

HERE WE GO.

MY DAD DOESN'T LET ME READ STUFF LIKE THAT.

--FOR EVERYONE ELSE.

I TAKE IT MAX PERFORMED WELL DURING HIS TESTS.

HE PASSED WITH FLYING COLORS.

MAX AND VIGO ARE THE BEST IN THEIR CLASS, BY A WIDE MARGIN.

PAT

ROY, I HOPE YOU'LL CONSIDER LETTING MAX SERVE ON THE GUARDIAN COUNCIL.

I DON'T OFTEN SEE YOUNG STONEKEEPERS WITH HIS LEVEL OF SKILL.

AFTER ALL, YOUR FATHER WAS A POWERFUL MEMBER OF THE COUNCIL HIMSELF.

WE WENT OVER THIS, ALREADY.

MAX WILL FOLLOW MY PATH, NOT MY FATHER'S.

WITH PROPER GUIDANCE, WE CAN HELP MAX BE A GREAT LEADER OF OUR PEOPLE.

PERHAPS FOR THE BEST.

WHERE ARE YOU GOING, MAX?

I'M MEETING WITH LAYRA.

YOU KNOW WHAT I SAID ABOUT SPENDING TIME WITH THAT FAMILY.

SHE'S MY FRIEND, DAD.

THEY SAID THIS WAS ONLY TEMPORARY.

THIS IS A BETRAYAL.

YEARS OF WORK HELPING THEM BUILD THEIR CITIES WITH ELF TECHNOLOGY AND THIS IS HOW THEY REPAY US.

MISTER JANUS, I'M HERE TO GET YOU OUT.

MAX?

IS LAYRA OKAY?

SHE'S FINE.

STAND BACK.

AND I'LL TAKE YOU TO HER.

MOM! DAD!

I WON'T LET THEM SEPARATE US AGAIN.

I ARRANGED FOR AN AIRSHIP TO TAKE YOU TO FRONTERA.

FROM THERE YOU CAN MAKE YOUR WAY SAFELY INTO GULFEN.

THANK YOU, MAX.

WELCOME ABOARD!

ARE YOU COMING WITH US?

I SHOULD STAY AND MAKE SURE NO ONE COMES AFTER YOU.

WE CAN MEET IN GULFEN.

THANKS, MAX.

I'LL SEE YOU SOON.

GET THEM TO FRONTERA AND DISAPPEAR.

DON'T STOP FOR ANYONE, UNDERSTAND?

I KNOW WHAT I'M DOING, KID.

16

17

18

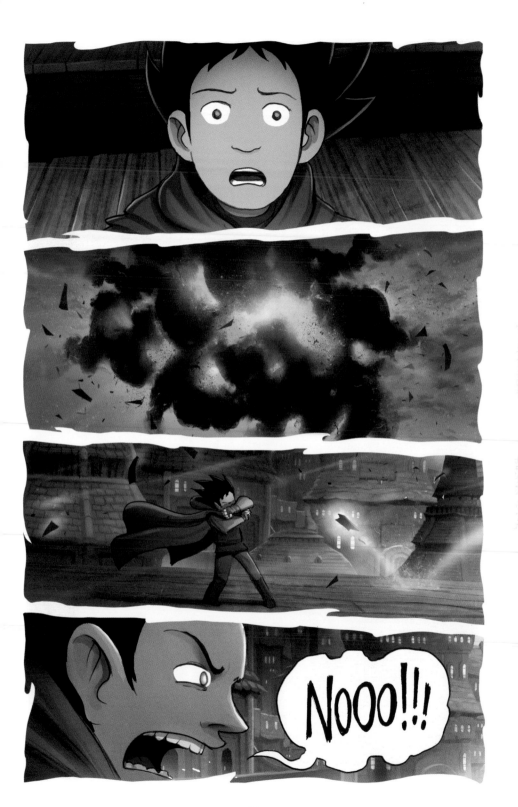

19

20

24

25

27

FIFTY YEARS LATER

HAVE YOU BEEN SITTING THERE ALL NIGHT, LOGI?

THE KING ASKED ME TO KEEP AN EYE ON YOU.

THE SUN ISN'T UP YET.

GATHER THE TROOPS.

WE START EARLY TODAY.

32

WE BOTH KNOW THAT ISN'T WHAT REALLY HAPPENED, TRAITOR.

YAAGH!

HUF HUF

IF ANYONE ELSE HAS SOMETHING TO SAY TO ME, SPEAK NOW.

OTHERWISE, YOU CAN TAKE YOUR COMPLAINTS DIRECTLY TO THE KING.

MY LOYALTY LIES WITH THE NATION OF ELVES.

QUESTION ME, AND I WILL ANSWER YOU WITH THE EDGE OF MY SWORD.

WHAT ARE WE GOING TO DO, CAPTAIN?

WHAT ANY GOOD SOLDIER IS SUPPOSED TO DO!

WE STAND OUR GROUND!

BUT WE'RE OUTNUMBERED!

HELLO, OLD FRIEND.

KRNK KRNK

YOUR MAJESTY.

WELCOME TO THE ICE PRISON OF KORTHAN.

TELL ME ABOUT THE PRISONER.

HIS NAME IS CHRONOS, A MOUNTAIN GIANT. ONE OF THE LAST OF HIS KIND.

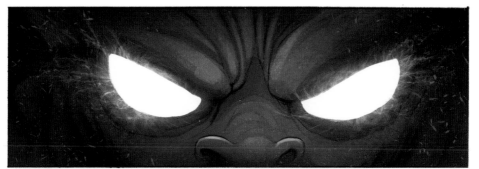

SOMEDAY YOU WILL BOTH SEE THAT THERE IS A LOT ABOUT YOUR PROGENITORS YOU DO NOT UNDERSTAND.

WHAT'S A PROGENITOR?

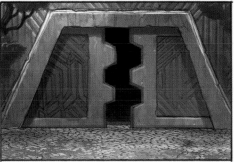

I FOUND SOMETHING I THINK YOU SHOULD SEE.

WHO ARE THESE PEOPLE, VIGO?

ARE THEY GHOSTS?

NOT QUITE.

THIS IS HOW THE COUNCIL RECORDS ITS MINUTES, AND STONEKEEPERS CAN ACCESS THE ARCHIVES.

I'VE BEEN HERE ALL NIGHT VIEWING THE COUNCIL'S FINAL MEETINGS.

IT'S BEEN INTERESTING SEEING WHAT TRANSPIRED AFTER I LEFT.

DID YOU FIND OUT WHAT HAPPENED TO THEM?

NO, NOT YET.

BUT PAY CAREFUL ATTENTION.

THIS FINAL TRANSMISSION IS WHAT I FELT YOU SHOULD SEE.

MAX.

SILAS.

VIGO, HOW OLD ARE THESE RECORDINGS?

THE ONE YOU'RE WATCHING IS OVER FIFTY YEARS OLD.

HOW IS THAT POSSIBLE?

THAT WOULD MAKE MAX OLDER THAN MY MOM.

I HEARD STONEKEEPERS CAN TRAVEL BACK IN TIME.

MAX MUST HAVE DISCOVERED HOW TO DO IT.

STONEKEEPERS CANNOT TRAVEL THROUGH TIME,

BUT THEY CAN ENTER THE VOID.

THE VOID IS A DREAMSPACE BUILT OF STONEKEEPER MEMORIES.

IT IS A PLACE WHERE STONEKEEPERS CAN GO TO EXAMINE THEIR PAST AND EVEN COMMUNICATE WITH ONE ANOTHER.

SILAS CHARNON ESPOUSED THE IDEA THAT THE VOID WAS REAL, AND IT COULD ALLOW YOU TO ALTER REALITY.

BUT HIS BELIEF WAS SHADOWED BY A DESIRE TO CHANGE THE EVENTS OF HIS PAST.

SOMETIMES, PERSONAL DESIRES AND AMBITIONS CAN CLOUD THE JUDGMENT OF EVEN OUR BRIGHTEST MINDS.

BUT WHAT DID SILAS DO THAT WAS SO WRONG?

HE ENCOURAGED YOUNG STONEKEEPERS TO ENTER THE VOID.

HE DID THIS WITHOUT TRULY UNDERSTANDING THE DANGERS THEY WOULD HAVE TO FACE.

OR THE PRICE THEY MIGHT ULTIMATELY PAY.

I WOULD PAY ANY PRICE TO FIX THE MISTAKES OF MY ANCESTORS.

YOU DON'T KNOW WHAT YOU ARE SAYING.

STAY OUT OF THIS.

I DO NOT KNOW HOW MAX HAS RETAINED HIS YOUTH, BUT I DID KNOW HIM ONCE.

HE WAS A STUDENT HERE AT THE ACADEMY.

WE WERE CLASSMATES.

IF WE ARE DEALING WITH THE SAME YOUNG MAN I KNEW BACK THEN --

-- OUR REAL TROUBLES HAVE ONLY JUST BEGUN.

HE'LL BE WITH YOU IN A MOMENT.

READY AND WAITING FOR HIM, MA'AM!

IF YOU NEED ANYTHING, JUST TELL THE ROBOT PEOPLE TO COME LOOK FOR ME, OKAY?

I'LL BE FINE.

I LOVE YOU.

I LOVE YOU TOO, MOM.

COMMANDER NAVIN,

I AM HONORED TO BE IN YOUR PRESENCE!

I CAN HARDLY BELIEVE OUR GOOD FORTUNE!

CAN I GET YOUR AUTOGRAPH?

UH, SURE.

BUT I DON'T SEE WHY YOU'D WANT IT.

I'M NOT FAMOUS OR ANYTHING.

ALL PILOTS ARE FAMOUS HERE!

WHAT A MARVELOUS TURN OF EVENTS THAT YOU ARRIVED JUST AS WE WERE GETTING READY TO REACTIVATE THE COLOSSUS!

YOU WERE SIMPLY DESTINED TO BE HERE!

AND NOW THE FATE OF OUR WORLD RESTS ON YOUR SHOULDERS!

HA HA!

THESE PEOPLE ARE CRAZY.

HEY, BILL!

THE PILOTS HAVE ARRIVED!

GOOD!

WE ARE IN NEED OF FRESH MEAT FOR THE WAR EFFORT!

NAMES, PLEASE.

MY NAME IS NAVIN.

AND THIS IS COGSLEY.

THEY'RE SHRIMPY, BUT THEY'LL DO.

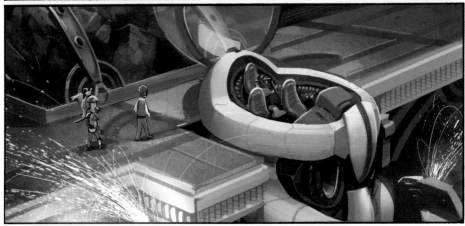

EVERYTHING HERE LOOKS FAMILIAR.

THAT'S NO ACCIDENT.

SILAS AND I DESIGNED HIS HOUSE TO EMULATE THE COLOSSUS.

SO YOU KNOW THESE CONTROLS, BUT THEY'RE MORE RESPONSIVE.

AND THIS MECH, UNLIKE THE CHARNON HOUSE, WAS BUILT FOR BATTLE.

LET'S SEE WHAT YOU CAN DO WITH THE REAL THING.

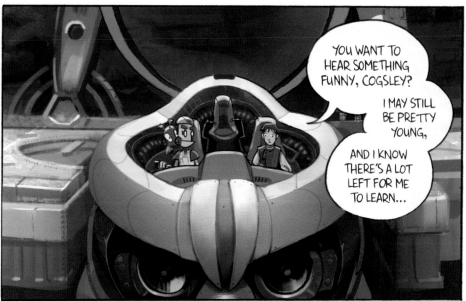

YOU WANT TO HEAR SOMETHING FUNNY, COGSLEY?

I MAY STILL BE PRETTY YOUNG,

AND I KNOW THERE'S A LOT LEFT FOR ME TO LEARN...

BUT I THINK THIS IS IT.

I THINK THIS IS WHAT I WAS MEANT TO DO WITH MY LIFE.

THAT WASN'T FUNNY AT ALL.

BY THE WAY,

DID YOU NOTICE THIS?

WE HAVE A THIRD SEAT.

MY NAME IS ALYSON HUNTER.

I'LL BE JOINING YOU IN THE NEW COLOSSUS PILOT PROGRAM.

HOW WAS I CHOSEN TO BE A PART OF THIS?

HONESTLY, YOU'RE THE ONLY ONE HERE WHO HAS BEEN TO BATTLE.

THE REST OF US HAVE ONLY TRAINED ON A SIMULATOR.

WELL, THAT'S KIND OF HOW I GOT STARTED, TOO.

HEY.

THAT'S MY SISTER.

YOUR SISTER AND VIGO LIGHT ARE WHAT REMAINS OF THE GUARDIAN COUNCIL.

SHE WILL NEED TO GUIDE US ALL INTO BATTLE.

IT'S A HEAVY BURDEN FOR SOMEONE HER AGE.

OUR JOB WILL BE TO PROVIDE HER WITH SUPPORT FROM THE CIELIS GUARD.

IS THIS THE YOUNG COMMANDER?

NAVIN, THIS IS MY DAD, CAPTAIN TRISTAN HUNTER.

NICE TO MEET YOU, SON.

I HEARD YOU HAD SOME EXPERIENCE OUT IN THE FIELD.

WE'RE GOING TO NEED EVERY OUNCE OF IT HERE.

I'M READY TO HELP IN ANY WAY I CAN.

THE CITY OF FRONTERA...

...IT'S GONE. THEY LEFT NOTHING BEHIND.

AND IT APPEARS MAX IS LEADING THEM.

THEIR NEXT MOVE WILL BE TO TAKE THE CITY OF LUCIEN.

LUCIEN'S ARMY IS FORMIDABLE, BUT THEY WILL BE OVERCOME.

IT WILL SIMPLY BE A MATTER OF TIME BEFORE THEY FALL.

THEN WE NEED TO SHOW THEM THAT THE GUARDIAN COUNCIL HAS RETURNED.

BUT YOU'VE SEEN THE STATE OF THINGS HERE.

WE ARE NOT READY.

WE'LL NEVER BE READY.

AND IF WE CHOOSE TO WAIT, WE'LL MISS OUR CHANCE TO MAKE A DIFFERENCE.

BROTHER, TELL ME MORE ABOUT HOW TO ACCESS EVENTS OF THE PAST.

THERE MUST BE A WAY I CAN LEARN TO DO THIS.

MASTERING THIS ABILITY WILL TAKE MANY YEARS, TRELLIS.

AND IT IS MUCH TOO DANGEROUS.

LISTEN TO THE OTHERS AND HEED THEIR WARNING.

STAY AWAY FROM SUCH DARK MAGIC.

WHY SHOULD I LISTEN TO THEM...

...WHEN THEY DON'T LISTEN TO ME?

THE SOLDIERS OF THE GUARD ARE ALL SO YOUNG.

ARE YOU SURE THEY'RE READY FOR THIS FIGHT?

WE ALL HAVE TO START SOMEWHERE.

WELCOME ABOARD, YOUR HIGHNESS!

ENZO!

DON'T CALL ME THAT!

I'M GLAD TO SEE YOU GUYS.

WOULDN'T MISS THIS FOR THE WORLD!

NOT EVERY DAY YOU GET ASKED TO ESCORT THE GUARDIAN COUNCIL!

NOW, WHERE'S YOUR LITTLE BROTHER?

NAVIN'S FLYING WITH THE OTHER COLOSSUS PILOTS.

IT WILL GIVE THEM SOME TIME TO GET ACQUAINTED.

COLOSSUS PILOT! WELL, WHADDYA KNOW.

THE LITTLE RUNT'S GRADUATED TO THE BIG TIME.

HE'S ALL GROWN-UP!

DO YOU WANT ME TO HOLD ON TO DAGNO?

I CAN KEEP HIM WITH ME IN THE CABIN.

THAT'S OKAY.

HE WON'T WANT TO LEAVE HIS MAMA'S SIDE.

LOOKS LIKE WE'RE FLYING CARGO CLASS!

STAY SAFE, COGSLEY.

SEE YOU IN LUCIEN, CHIEF!

TRELLIS, AT LEAST LET THE OTHERS KNOW.

I REALLY FEEL THAT YOU SHOULDN'T DO THIS.

AND WHY NOT, BROTHER?

DO YOU NOT WANT TO FIX OUR PAST?

WE NEED TO UNDERSTAND IT BEFORE WE CAN REPAIR IT.

AND IF SOMETHING WERE TO GO WRONG,

I WOULDN'T BE ABLE TO COME HELP YOU.

HAS YOUR DAD ALWAYS PUT SO MUCH TRUST IN YOU?

YEAH.

I GUESS HE HAS.

IT MUST BE NICE TO HAVE YOUR DAD CLOSE BY.

HE MAKES ME FEEL MORE CONFIDENT.

HE ALWAYS TOLD ME TO IMAGINE THE KIND OF PERSON I THOUGHT OF AS A HERO --

-- AND BE THAT PERSON.

I THINK I WANT TO BE LIKE YOUR DAD.

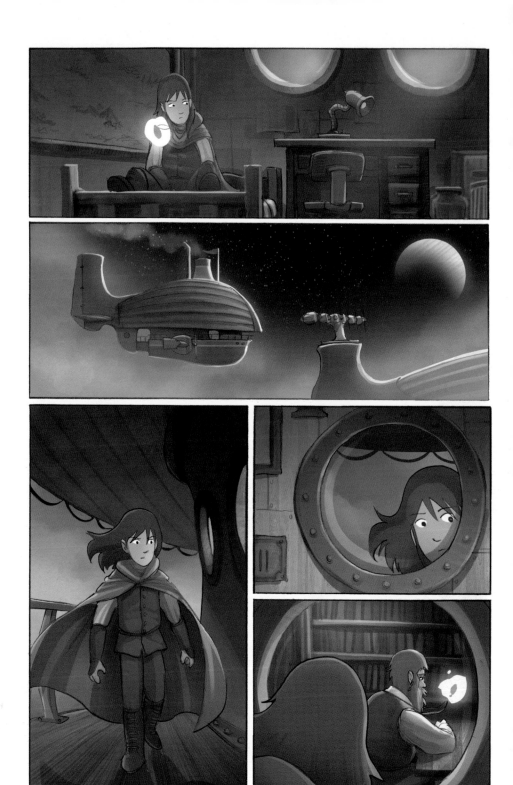

THIS WAS AROUND THE TIME
SILAS BEGAN LECTURING ABOUT
THE POSSIBILITIES OF TIME
TRAVEL USING THE STONES.

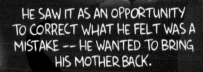

I SHOULD HAVE REALIZED
THAT DANIEL WAS BECOMING
MORE INTERESTED IN THE IDEA
THAN THE OTHER STUDENTS.

HE SAW IT AS AN OPPORTUNITY
TO CORRECT WHAT HE FELT WAS A
MISTAKE -- HE WANTED TO BRING
HIS MOTHER BACK.

USING HIS POWERS, DANIEL
ATTEMPTED TO TRAVEL BACK
TO SAVE HIS MOTHER.

BUT HE ONLY WENT
INTO A DEEP SLEEP, AND
DID NOT WAKE FOR DAYS.

I SAT AT HIS BEDSIDE
WHILE HE SPOKE TO
SOMEONE IN HIS
SLEEP.

WHEN HE FINALLY
OPENED HIS EYES, HE
LOOKED TERRIFIED.

THEN HE
WAS GONE.

SOON AFTER THAT, THE STONE RETURNED ITSELF TO ME.

WHO WAS HE TALKING TO?

I ASSUMED DANIEL BELIEVED HE WAS TALKING TO HIS MOTHER.

BUT HE SPOKE ABOUT THINGS HE NEVER WOULD HAVE WITH HER.

THAT'S WHEN I REALIZED HE WAS SPEAKING TO THE STONE.

I WISHED HE FELT HE COULD TALK TO ME INSTEAD OF TURNING TO HIS IMAGINARY FRIENDS FOR HELP.

THAT'S NO
WYVERN.

BOOM!

99

VRRRRRR

100

HEY, CHIEF!

DON'T LEAVE US STRANDED HERE, OKAY?

WE STILL HAVE A LOT OF WORK TO DO!

I'LL BE RIGHT BACK, COGSLEY.

NAVIN, TEST THE WINGS.

THESE SILVERHAWKS HAVEN'T BEEN FLOWN IN A WHILE.

DROP ON MY MARK!

VRRRRRNN

THREE...

TWO...

...ONE!!

KCHUNG!

KCHUNG!

VWOM!!

HE JUST STOPPED IT!

PULL UP, NAVIN! TAKE US UP!!!

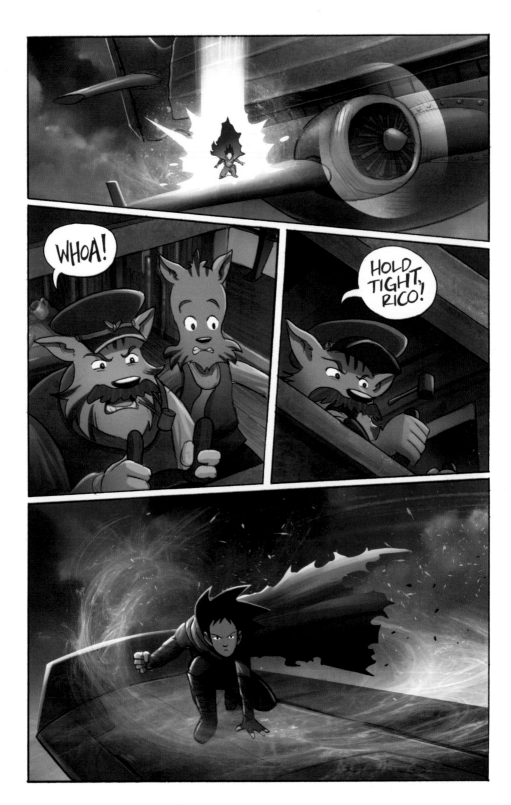

ALL OF MY TARGETS IN ONE PLACE.

WHAT KIND OF STRATEGY IS THIS?!

I HONESTLY EXPECTED MORE FROM THE BOTH OF YOU.

HE CAN'T TAKE US BOTH DOWN AT ONCE.

HE WILL HAVE TO CHOOSE.

READY WHEN YOU ARE, VIGO.

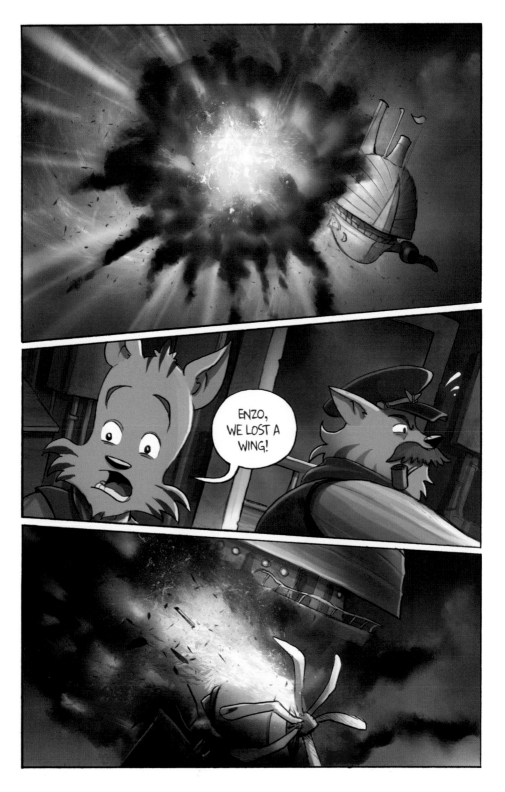

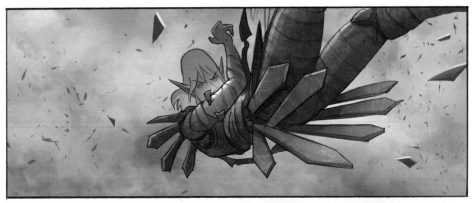

WHY ARE YOU FOLLOWING ME?

MY BROTHER TOLD ME NOT TO TALK WITH YOU.

YOU'LL WANT TO SPEAK WITH UNCLE VIRGIL.

HE'S THE ONE WHO FOUND YOU AND MENDED YOUR ARM.

HIS HOUSE IS ON THE OTHER SIDE OF THE POND.

YOU WON'T HAVE TO KNOCK.

HE IS ALREADY EXPECTING YOU.

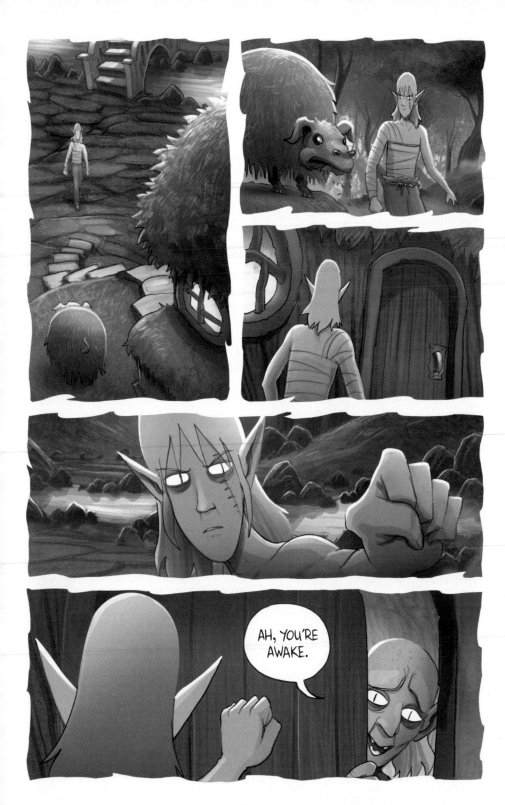

LET ME GET YOU A SHIRT.

YOU MUST BE FREEZING.

I LOOKED UP AND SAW YOU FALL OUT OF THE SKY.

IT'S A TRUE MIRACLE THAT YOU WERE ABLE TO SURVIVE.

I THOUGHT YOU DIED.

WHERE IS EVERYONE?

POOR BOY, YOU MUST BE DELIRIOUS.

WHEN YOU FELL, YOU WERE QUITE ALONE.

I HAVE TO GO AND FIND MY FRIENDS. THEY NEED MY HELP.

I SWEAR NO ONE WAS WITH YOU.

I STILL NEED TO SEE FOR MYSELF.

THANK YOU... FOR EVERYTHING.

TRELLIS!

LUGER?

WHAT DID I TELL YOU, TRELLIS?

FSK!

PEOPLE WILL COME AND ASK QUESTIONS ABOUT DAD.

YOU MUST NOT TALK TO THEM.

DON'T WORRY, LUGER.

I WASN'T TALKING WITH HIM.

HE WASN'T ASKING ABOUT DAD, ANYWAY.

WHO ARE YOU?

WE KNOW EVERYBODY ON THIS ISLAND.

AND I HAVE NEVER SEEN YOU HERE BEFORE.

STAY AWAY FROM UNCLE VIRGIL.

FATHER WILL DEAL WITH HIM LATER.

DON'T MIND MY NEPHEW LUGER.

HE'S UNDER A LOT OF PRESSURE NOW THAT HIS FATHER IS THE KING.

WHY ARE YOU HELPING ME?

SOMETHING TELLS ME THAT IT'S MY DUTY TO HELP.

AND UNLIKE MANY OF THE ELVES ON THIS ISLAND,

I HAVE A VERY GOOD SENSE OF WHO I NEED TO TRUST.

133

YOU MENTIONED YOU WANTED ME TO HELP YOU SORT SOME BOOKS.

I WOULD LIKE TO REPAY YOU SOMEHOW.

GOOD!

HOP IN THE BOAT AND WE'LL BE ON OUR WAY.

THE LIBRARY IS LOCATED IN THE MIDDLE OF THE LAKE.

I THINK YOU'LL LIKE IT THERE.

UT PUT PUT PUT PUT

PUT PUT PUT PUT PUT PUT

WITH SO MANY ELVES BEING DRAFTED FOR THE WAR, IT'S BEEN HARD TO FIND GOOD HELP.

YOU CAME AT A GOOD TIME.

THIS LIBRARY WAS BUILT TO HONOR THAT TRADITION.

THE BOOKS CONTAINED WITHIN THESE WALLS DOCUMENT THE MANY LIVES WHO HAVE DEDICATED THEMSELVES TO FURTHERING THE ADVANCEMENT OF ELFKIND.

IT IS HOW WE HAVE PROGRESSED FASTER THAN ALL OTHER SETTLERS ON ALLEDIAN SOIL.

IT'S MOST UNFORTUNATE FOR THIS CURRENT GENERATION THAT MY BROTHER IS NOT AN AVID READER OF HISTORY.

IF HE WAS, HE WOULD SEE ALL THE WARNING SIGNS.

WARNING SIGNS?

HISTORY HAS A TENDENCY TO REPEAT ITSELF.

CAN I GET ANYTHING FOR YOU, MASTER VIRGIL?

THANK YOU, LOGI.

BUT WE'D RATHER BE LEFT TO OURSELVES.

YES, OF COURSE.

I'VE BEEN VERY CONCERNED WITH THE DIRECTION THIS WAR IS HEADED.

WITH JUST A QUICK GLANCE AT OUR HISTORY, I BEGAN TO UNDER-STAND WHY.

I RECENTLY FOUND SOMETHING VERY INTERESTING IN A BOOK ABOUT OUR PAST KINGS.

AH, GOOD. IT'S STILL HERE.

LEVITAS. THE FOURTH KING.

HE BECAME AN ENDURING HISTORICAL FIGURE FOR TWO REASONS.

THE FIRST WAS HIS PENCHANT FOR CONFLICT THAT SENT US INTO A CIVIL WAR.

HIS RULE MARKS THE DEADLIEST PERIOD IN ELF HISTORY.

THE SECOND WAS THAT MANY PEOPLE CLAIMED HE WAS POSSESSED BY HIS STONE.

THEY SAY HE SPOKE TO IT.

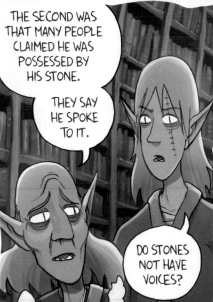

DO STONES NOT HAVE VOICES?

THE STONE IS A MEDIUM, NOT A MESSENGER.

LET ME SHOW YOU SOMETHING.

OH, GOOD.

I HID THIS ONE WELL.

I SEARCHED EVERY WING IN THIS LIBRARY FOR ANOTHER MENTION OF THE VOICE, AND I CAME UP EMPTY...

...UNTIL I FOUND THIS BOOK.

THE AUTHOR IS HUMAN, AND HE BELIEVES THAT THE STONE-SHARD AMULETS WERE CREATED TO PROVIDE THE STONEKEEPERS WITH THREE THINGS:

POWER, COMMUNICATION, AND TRAVEL.

THE AMULET GRANTS ITS KEEPER THE ABILITY TO WIELD THE KINETIC ENERGY OF THE MOTHER STONE.

BUT IT ALSO GRANTS THEM THE ABILITY TO COMMUNICATE AND TO TRAVEL USING A PLANE OF EXISTENCE PARALLEL TO OUR OWN.

WHEN THEY DO, STONEKEEPERS MAY FIND THEMSELVES UNDER THE INFLUENCE OF A DARK, GOVERNING SPIRIT -- A "VOICE."

WHY DOES THIS INTEREST YOU, VIRGIL?

BECAUSE MY BROTHER SPEAKS TO HIS STONE.

AND YOU BELIEVE HE IS SPEAKING TO THIS DARK SPIRIT?

LOOK AT THIS.

THE VOICE APPEARS EVERY TIME THE ELVES ENTER A TIME OF WAR AND STRIFE.

THIS IS FOLLOWED BY 500 YEARS OF PEACE BEFORE THE CYCLE BEGINS ANEW.

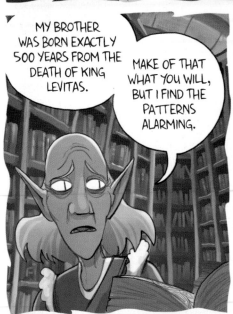

MY BROTHER WAS BORN EXACTLY 500 YEARS FROM THE DEATH OF KING LEVITAS.

MAKE OF THAT WHAT YOU WILL, BUT I FIND THE PATTERNS ALARMING.

FLIP
FLIP
FLIP

VIRGIL--

WHERE DID YOU GET THIS?

On Stone Power
by
Silas Charnon

IF THE KING FINDS THIS BOOK HE WILL HAVE YOU EXECUTED!

WHY ARE YOU TRUSTING ME WITH THIS INFORMATION?!

I'M TRUSTING YOU BECAUSE YOU NEED TO KNOW ALL OF THIS.

YOU NEED TO TAKE THIS KNOWLEDGE BACK WITH YOU.

YOU KNOW WHO I AM?

I RAISED YOU, TRELLIS.

I WOULD RECOGNIZE YOU NO MATTER HOW OLD OR YOUNG YOU WERE.

I CAME BACK TO TRY AND FIX THINGS.

IT'S BETTER THAT YOU FOCUS ON DOING WHAT'S RIGHT FOR THE FUTURE.

145

148

GET UP,
TRELLIS!

HOW DID
YOU FIND
ME?

HOW DID YOU
KNOW WHERE I
WOULD BE IN
THE PAST?

WE'RE NOT
IN THE PAST,
TRELLIS.

WE'RE IN YOUR
MEMORIES!

AND I NEED
YOU TO WAKE
UP FROM THIS
DREAM!

A DREAM?

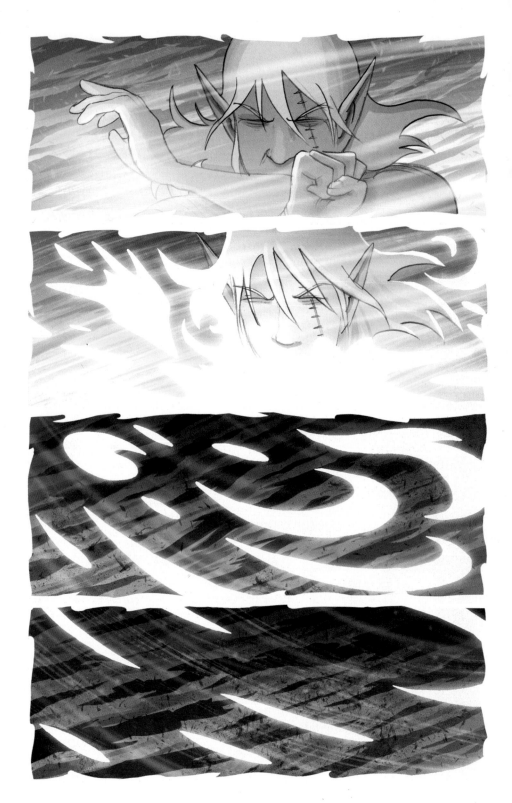

EMILY,
WAKE UP.

EMILY.

I KNOW
HOW I CAN
HELP NOW.

THANK YOU FOR COMING TO GET ME.

EMILY WOKE YOU FROM THE VOID?

YES, BUT WHY IS SHE STILL ASLEEP?

SHE MUST STILL BE INSIDE.

HER BREATHING SEEMS REGULAR.

SHE'S IN CONTROL.

THAT MEANS SHE'S STILL ALIVE.

HOW DO WE WAKE HER UP?

YOU'RE THE REASON SHE'S IN THERE.

SO YOU'RE GOING BACK THERE TO GET HER OUT.

AND HOW DO I GET US BOTH BACK SAFELY?

WE WOULD NOT BE STANDING HERE IF YOU DIDN'T KNOW WHAT TO DO, TRELLIS.

WHERE ARE WE?

WE'RE NEAR THE ICE PRISON OF KORTHAN.

IS THIS YOUR MEMORY?

NO.

LOOK.

MAX.

HE MUST BE DREAMING ABOUT THIS NEARBY.

I ENTERED EASILY, SO HE'S ALSO WEAK.

I'M HERE TO BRING YOU BACK.

WE SHOULD GO BEFORE--

WAIT.

YOUR TIME IS RUNNING OUT, MAX.

IF YOU GIVE UP, LAYRA WILL HAVE DIED FOR NOTHING.

KOF! KOF!

IF YOU DIE, YOU WILL LET THEM WIN.

GIVE ME CONTROL AND WE CAN MAKE THEM PAY.

I...

...AM...

...YOURS...

THANK
YOU.

SHK!

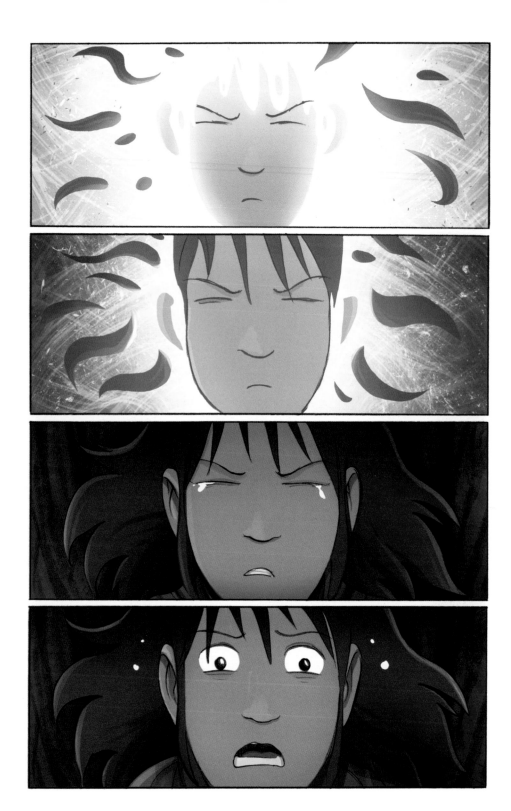

EMILY!

YOU LIED TO ME!!!

YOU HEARD THE VOICE.

WHY DIDN'T YOU TELL ME, EMILY?

TRELLIS--

IF WE WORK TOGETHER, WE'LL STOP HIM.

WHAT IF THAT'S PART OF HIS PLAN?

THERE THEY ARE, NAVIN!

EM!

I THOUGHT YOU WERE GONE.

I WOULD NEVER LET THAT HAPPEN TO YOU.

YOU FELLAS GOT OUT OKAY?

WE'RE A LITTLE BANGED UP BUT WE'RE STILL IN BUSINESS!

PUTTING IN THIS SPARE ENGINE HAS ALREADY PAID OFF!

THANKS FOR COMING BACK TO GET ME.

LET'S JUST SAY WE'RE EVEN.

NNGHH...

STAND UP, MAX.

YOU HAVE MORE WORK TO DO.

I... I CAN'T MOVE...

I THINK...
...MY BONES...
...ARE BROKEN.

AGH!

SH-KRIK!

SH-KRAK!!

PLEASE, STOP!

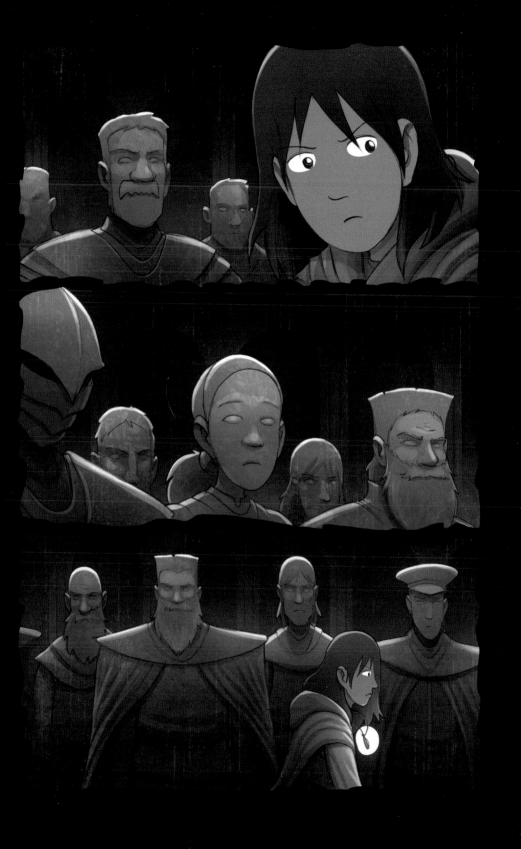

END OF BOOK FIVE

CREATED AT

BOLT CITY
PRODUCTIONS
IN ALHAMBRA, CALIFORNIA

WRITTEN AND ILLUSTRATED BY
KAZU KIBUISHI

LEAD PRODUCTION ARTIST
JASON CAFFOE

COLORS & BACKGROUND
JASON CAFFOE
ZANE YARBROUGH
CHRYSTIN GARLAND
KAZU KIBUISHI

PAGE FLATTING
MARY CAGLE
KELLY McCLELLAN
STUART LIVINGSTON
DENVER JACKSON
MEGAN BRENNAN
JON CHUAN JU LEE

SPECIAL THANKS

Gordon & Lydia & Ellie Luk, Amy & Juni Kim Kibuishi, Judy Hansen, David Saylor, Phil Falco, Cassandra Pelham, Ben Zhu & the Gallery Nucleus crew, Nick & Melissa Harris, Nancy Caffoe, the Flight artists, Tao & Taka & Tyler Kibuishi, Tim Ganter, Rachel Ormiston, Khang Le & Adhesive Games, June & Masa & Julie & Emi Kibuishi, Sheila Marie Everett, Lizette Serrano, Bess Braswell, Whitney Steller, Lori Benton, and Ellie Berger.

And the biggest thanks of all to the librarians, booksellers, parents, and readers who have supported us all these years. You mean the world to us.

ABOUT THE AUTHOR

Kazu Kibuishi is the founder and editor of the acclaimed Flight anthologies and is also the creator of *Copper*, a collection of his popular webcomic that features an adventuresome boy-and-dog pair. *Amulet, Book One: The Stonekeeper* was an ALA Best Book for Young Adults and a Children's Choice Book Award finalist. The second, third, and fourth books in the Amulet series, *The Stonekeeper's Curse*, *The Cloud Searchers*, and *The Last Council*, were all *New York Times* bestsellers. Kazu lives and works in Alhambra, California, with his wife and fellow comics artist, Amy Kim Kibuishi, and their son.

Visit Kazu online at www.boltcity.com.

WINDSOR
Ice Prison of Korthan
Gondoa Mountain
NOBUO RANGE
TAKA RIVER
Kanalis
Demon's Head Mountain
Black Forest
Gorbon
Nautilus
Drucker Canyon
COCONINO MOUNTAINS
COCONINO VALLEY
Pomo
LUFEN

OTHER GRAPHIC
NOVELS BY
KAZU KIBUISHI

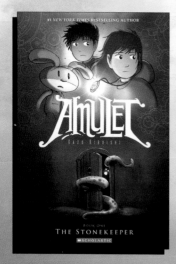

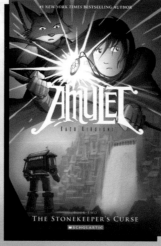

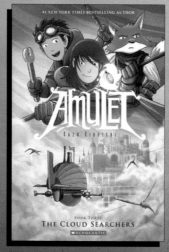

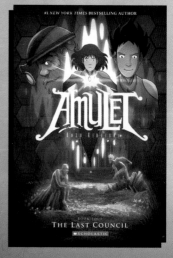